The Library of PIRATES™

Henry Morgan

Seventeenth-Century Buccaneer

Aileen Weintraub

The Rosen Publishing Group's
PowerKids Press™
New York

To my DaddyMonster, who was the most fearless of them all

Published in 2002 by The Rosen Publishing Group, Inc.
29 East 21st Street, New York, NY 10010

First Edition

Project Editors: Jennifer Landau, Jason Moring, Jennifer Quasha
Book Design: Michael Caroleo and Michael de Guzman
Layout: Colin Dizengoff

Photo Credits: pp. 4 (Morgan), 8 (buccaneer), 11, 12 © Mary Evans Picture Library; p. 4 (map) © Michael Maslan Historic Photographs/CORBIS; pp. 7, 19 illustrations by Mica Angela Fulgium; p. 8 (treasure) © Jeffrey L. Rotman/CORBIS; p. 15 © The Art Archive/Eileen Tweedy; p. 16 © North Wind Pictures; p. 20 © Bettmann/CORBIS.

Weintraub, Aileen, 1973–
Henry Morgan : seventeenth-century buccaneer / Aileen Weintraub.
    p. cm. — (The library of pirates)
    Includes bibliographical references (p.   ).
    ISBN 0–8239–5798–5 (lib. bdg.)
    1. Morgan, Henry, Sir, 1635?–1688—Juvenile literature. 2. Caribbean Area—Description and travel—Juvenile literature. 3. Portobello (Panama)—History—Juvenile literature. 4. Buccaneers—Biography—Juvenile literature. 5. Governors—Jamaica—Biography—Juvenile literature. [1. Morgan, Henry, Sir, 1635?–1688. 2. Buccaneers. 3. Pirates. 4. Caribbean Area.] I. Title.
F2161.M83 W45 2002
972.92'03'092—dc21

                                                                                        00–013040

Manufactured in the United States of America

Contents

Left: *The map shows the coasts of South America.*
Right: *Henry Morgan never thought of himself as a pirate.*

A Young Soldier

Sir Henry Morgan was one of the most famous **buccaneers** of all time. He **raided** ships and towns along the Spanish Main during the seventeenth century. The Spanish Main was a term used to describe Central and South America and, in time, the Caribbean. Morgan usually had the support of the British government. He would raid ships that belonged to England's enemies and keep part of the treasure as payment.

Some governments did not want to pay for navies to attack enemy ships. Instead governments would permit pirates to do this.

Henry Morgan was born in Wales in 1635. Little is known of his early life other than that two of his uncles were soldiers. In the 1650s, Morgan joined the British army to help England fight against the Spanish.

Morgan's First Fight

In 1654, Morgan was fighting the Spanish under the command of the British general Venables and **Admiral** Penn. These men wanted to take over the Spanish island of Hispaniola. Seven thousand men landed on the south side of the island at Santo Domingo. The Spanish fought hard against the British troops. Many of the British came down with **tropical** diseases and died. The British were not organized and did not have strong leaders. The Spanish defeated them. Penn and Venables decided to attack the weak island of Jamaica. They took over the island, making it a British settlement. The island became a port for both **privateers** and the British navy. Morgan spent the following years raiding towns in Central America.

This picture shows Henry Morgan (left) fighting against the Spanish on Hispaniola.

These gold and silver coins were found in the wreck of a Spanish ship lost off the Bahamas in the seventeenth century.

Right: *This picture shows a buccaneer in 1686. The term buccaneer comes from the French word* boucan, *meaning "strips of smoked meat."*

King of the Buccaneers

Morgan soon became known as a successful military leader. In 1662, he commanded a ship that attacked Santiago de Cuba. He led another raid in which he **plundered** Gran Grenada, in Nicaragua.

By 1665, Henry Morgan was married to his cousin, Dame Mary Elizabeth. The Morgans lived in Jamaica. The buccaneers gave Henry Morgan the title Admiral **Brethren** of the Coast. This meant he was now considered a leader of pirates and privateers.

Morgan decided to attack Puerto del Principe in Cuba. He stole 50,000 **pieces of eight** during this raid. This money was not enough to satisfy his men. Morgan's next attack would be one of the most famous in history.

A Famous Attack

The Spanish had a treasure port called Portobello. This port held a lot of gold and riches. This port was on the northern coast of the Isthmus of Panama. Morgan knew that the forts in Portobello weren't well guarded. In July 1668, Morgan sailed with 12 ships and 500 men to an island west of Portobello. There the men switched to canoes and quietly rowed to Portobello. They arrived before dawn on July 11.

The buccaneers planned to surprise the men guarding the town. There were only five guards, but when they saw the buccaneers they fired their guns. This alarmed everyone in the town. Suddenly there was confusion and fear. Morgan's plan to surprise the island had failed.

This picture shows Morgan attacking the Spanish in Panama. Pirates often used short swords called cutlasses as weapons. ▶

This picture by artist Howard Pyle shows Henry Morgan taking over the city of Portobello.

The Taking of Portobello

Morgan's soldiers ran to the castle in Portobello. They hoped to find a lot of treasure there. Morgan ordered his men to charge the castle. One group ran into the town and killed anyone in their way. They locked many people in the town church. Then Morgan captured the mayor of the town, some women, **friars**, and nuns. He used these people as a human shield. Some soldiers of the town fired at the buccaneers from within the castle. Two friars were wounded and a buccaneer was killed. After that no more shots were fired. Morgan entered the castle. The man in charge of weapons for the soldiers in Portobello asked Morgan's men to shoot him. He felt responsible for the town being attacked. The buccaneers fulfilled his wish and killed him. Morgan then had control of Portobello.

A Ransom for a City

After taking over Portobello, Morgan sent a letter to Don Agustin, the president of Panama. Morgan wrote he would burn Portobello if he didn't get a large amount of money, called a **ransom**. At first the president refused to take the letter. He then sent an army of 800 men to Portobello to drive away Morgan and his men. The journey was difficult and most men didn't make it. After three weeks, Don Agustin agreed to pay the ransom. Morgan soon had a treasure of gold and silver. He also had all the **booty** he had stolen from the town. Morgan was given a hero's welcome when he returned home to Jamaica. The capture of Portobello went down in history as one of the most successful raids of the seventeenth century.

This drawing by artist Eileen Tweedy shows Morgan celebrating after his arrival in Jamaica. ▶

Morgan's Luck

By October 1668, Morgan and his men had run out of money. They planned another raid and sailed to Isla Vaca on the southwestern coast of Hispaniola. By January 1669, Morgan had 10 ships and about 900 men. Morgan and his men decided to raid the city of Cartagena, on the Spanish Main. The night this was decided, the men had a big party to celebrate. At some point during the celebration, it is believed that a candle was knocked over on Morgan's ship. The flames set off the gunpowder on board and blew apart the ship. Morgan was one of only 10 people who survived the blast. Two to three hundred others died. The raid had to be called off.

◄ *This picture shows Morgan's ship, the Oxford, in flames. The ship caught fire after a candle was knocked over.*

A New Plan

After Morgan's ship blew up, he needed a new plan. He sailed to the coast of Venezuela. Admiral Alonso, of Spain's West Indian fleet, heard about this and set a trap for Morgan. Admiral Alonso blocked the channel so Morgan couldn't pass through it. Morgan learned of the plan. He disguised a captured Cuban ship to look like a warship. The ship was loaded with gunpowder. Morgan secretly managed to attach this ship to a Spanish ship. He lit a **fuse**. Before the men on the Spanish ship knew what was happening, both ships exploded. Then Morgan tricked the soldiers into thinking he was going to attack by land. The Spanish soldiers moved to cover the land. In the middle of the night, Morgan escaped from the Spanish by sea.

Morgan dressed logs as buccaneers to make his ship look like a warship.

The Battle Between ye Spaniards and Pirates or Buccaneers Before the City of PANAMA

Spain Declares War

The British government gave Morgan the title of admiral and named him **commander in chief** of all the warships in Jamaica. Spain was angry that Morgan was attacking their land. They declared war on Jamaica. On January 28, 1671, Morgan took over Spanish-owned Panama. Britain was not pleased with Morgan's actions. Britain was at peace with Spain, so Morgan had no right to attack the Spanish. The Spanish wanted Morgan to pay for his crimes. In April 1672, Morgan was arrested and sent back to England. He spent two years in London but was never thrown in prison. As a matter of fact, he was treated very well in London.

◄ *This picture shows Henry Morgan's attack on Spanish Panama in 1671. Morgan found very little treasure because the people of Panama had already hidden it.*

The Death of Morgan

In 1674, the governor of Jamaica was replaced. King Charles II of England not only appointed Morgan the new assistant to the governor, but he also **knighted** the buccaneer. This was a very high honor and meant that Morgan would then be known as Sir Henry Morgan. Morgan went back to Jamaica in March 1676. He did not get along with the governor. After some time, Morgan proved he was a strong leader and became the acting governor when the real governor could not perform his duties.

Morgan became very ill, suffering from a disease called **dropsy**. He did not take good care of himself and died in 1688. He was given a noble burial. It is said that the sound of ships firing their guns out of respect for this fearless leader could be heard far and wide.

Glossary

admiral (AD-muh-rul) A naval officer of the highest rank.

booty (BOO-tee) Prizes stolen by force.

brethren (BRETH-ren) Members of a certain group or society.

buccaneers (buh-kuh-NEERZ) Pirates who practiced piracy along the Spanish coast in the seventeenth century.

commander in chief (kuh-MAN-dur IN CHEEF) The person in charge of all of the armed forces.

dropsy (DRAHP-see) An old name for an illness in which a person gets an unhealthy amount of liquid buildup in his or her cells and tissues.

friars (FRY-urz) Brothers in a communal religious order.

fuse (FYOOZ) A wick or tube filled with something that can be lit to cause a flame or fire.

knighted (NYT-id) Named a member of a special group of soliders.

pieces of eight (PEES-es UV AYT) Gold coins used by pirates.

plundered (PLUN-derd) To have robbed by force.

privateers (pry-vuh-TEERZ) Armed pirates licensed by the government to attack enemy ships.

raided (RAYD-id) To have suddenly attacked or invaded.

ransom (RAN-sum) Money paid, or terms met, so that a prisoner will be set free.

tropical (TRAH-pih-kul) Having to do with the warm parts of Earth that are near the equator.

Index

Web Sites

To learn more about Henry Morgan, check out this Web site: www.data-wales.co.uk/morgan.htm